I0785438

WRITE TO MARKET

How to Write your Book Faster and Get It Published

© Copyright 2017 - All rights reserved.

The contents of this book may not be reproduced, duplicated, or transmitted without direct written permission from the author.

Under no circumstances will any legal responsibility or blame be held against the publisher for any reparation, damages, or monetary loss due to the information herein, either directly or indirectly.

Legal Notice:

This book is copyright protected. This is only for personal use. You cannot amend, distribute, sell, use, quote or paraphrase any part or the content within this book without the consent of the author.

Disclaimer Notice:

Please note the information contained within this document is for educational and entertainment purposes only. Every attempt has been made to provide accurate, up to date and reliable complete information. No warranties of any kind are expressed or implied. Readers acknowledge that the author is not engaging in the rendering of legal, financial, medical or professional advice. The content of this book has been derived from various sources. Please consult a licensed professional before attempting any techniques outlined in this book.

By reading this document, the reader agrees that under no circumstances are is the author responsible for any losses, direct or indirect, which are incurred because of the use of information contained within this document, including, but not limited to, —errors, omissions, or inaccuracies.

TABLE OF CONTENTS

Before you continue, do you want a free book that teaches you how to earn even more money?

If you answered YES, you're in the right place. Nowadays, everyone needs a little help making ends meet. The methods described in this book will work for anyone willing to put in the effort. But once rolling, passive income can be a ticket to the financial freedom you've always wanted. No more living paycheck to paycheck. No more scrounging for extra cash after the bills are paid. With the tools described in this book, it is possible to live debt free and even quit your full-time job.

Right now, you can get a FREE copy of Passive Recurring Income with Shopify. This book gives you all the tools you need to supplement your income. Go to this link to instant access: https://nicholalett.lpages.co/passive-income/

CHAPTER ONE

INTRODUCTION

Writing a book can seem like a daunting task. There are so many details to keep up with, especially when navigating the complexities of the publishing industry. Luckily, the process can be simplified through careful planning and a little bit of organization. Organization and having a plan in place for writing a book will not only help you to write faster it will also allow you to reach your end goals.

As you begin the process of writing your book, you need to decide what type of book you would like to write. Whether you choose fiction or non-fiction will be entirely dependent upon your tastes and the topic you want to write about. After you've chosen what kind of book you want to write, you'll need to come up with an outline. The outline will help you stay organized and keep you on track as you work through the writing process.

Once you have chosen the type of book you want to write and outlined the details of the book, you'll need to focus on character development. Character development will be a crucial part of your story. Even in non-fiction writing, choosing the right voice for the piece will keep your reader engaged and focused on the information you are providing.

After you have carefully laid out a working plan, writing the book will be a lot easier. If you prefer, you can even hire a ghostwriter to fill in the actual details. Then, the technical work begins. Editing, formatting, creating a book cover, and marketing will all follow in the technical process to finalize your book. Depending on whether or not you choose to self-publish or go through a publishing service provider will dictate the extent of work needed on your end in each of these categories. Some publishers provide these services in exchange for a portion of your royalties. Others may require an upfront sum of money. In either case, you should weigh the benefits of the services they're providing against the anticipated revenue from your book before deciding.

The entire process can seem overwhelming for someone who is new to writing. That's why it's important to understand each step of the process and make sure that you feel comfortable and confident in making decisions for your book. Starting with a well thought out plan and listing out your goals in the beginning will save you time and energy later. It will also enable you to keep track of your progress as you move towards a finished product. With the help of this guide, you'll be able to perfect your writing skills and have a process that is both effective and efficient.

Chapter Two
Getting Started

There are several steps involved in writing a well-crafted book. Before you can begin writing, you first need to figure out what kind of book you want to write. Your book will generally fall into one of two categories: fiction or non-fiction. There are pluses and minuses to each category and depending on your personal tastes and what you are trying to accomplish with your book will determine whether or not your book will be a work of fiction or non-fiction. To begin, we'll cover the basics of both fiction and non-fiction books and the important things to consider with each category.

Using imaginary people or scenarios is what is known as fiction. Sometimes, fiction is based off real life events, but maybe exaggerated to tell a story or make a point. Fiction can be difficult to write for some because it usually requires a lot of creativity. Sometimes, fictional stories involve building an entire world for the reader and coming up with clever story ideas. You can use inspiration that you find from everyday events to help you come up with a story idea. If you find that you are stuck on deciding what you want to write about or where you want your story to go, try taking a break and just focus on your day-to-day activities. You might be surprised to find that something as simple as a dinner conversation can serve as your inspiration for your next book. When all else fails, write what you know. If you enjoy romance, fantasy, or sci-fi, use those interests to your advantage and work in your everyday inspirations to create a unique and one of a kind story.

Non-fiction focuses on true events. It could be an instruction manual, a real-life experience, a how-to guide, or a reference book that you want to write about. These fall into the non-fiction category. When writing non-fiction, you will pull from information that either you possess or information from research that you've conducted. Non-fiction doesn't have to be stiff or formal writing. It can be engaging and captivate readers just as much as works of fiction. It's important to pull your reader into your book. One of the ways that you can do this with non-fiction is by using your own voice to tell your story. Instead of regurgitating information, try to present it in a way that's new and fresh. Take a personal approach when possible and speak directly to the reader. This creates an engaging connection that will keep the reader's interest long after they've found the information they were looking for.

Finding the Right Niche

The key to being successful whether you're writing fiction or non-fiction is by finding the perfect niche. You can start the process by thinking about things you are passionate about. This will help you to be more motivated to produce better writing. Your passion will show in your writing and keep your readers interested and invested in your work. Make a list of the topics that inspire you. You can use this list as you research each topic to find which one will yield the highest return.

After you have your list of topics or ideas, research what is currently popular and be on the look out for up and coming ideas. Some of the ways to figure out what's currently driving the market is to look at the genre you've selected. If it's a how-to book, go to Amazon and look up other how to books. Amazon offers a variety of categories and book rankings that will give you an idea of how successful a book has been. Review those subcategories and see what's selling under each heading. You can do this for any genre. Click a similar book to the one you're thinking about writing and review the 'product details' section. You'll find the Amazon's Best Sellers Rank that will compare how well the book is selling in the overall market as well as the books ranking in each subcategory. You can click the subcategory and see what kinds of books are at the top of that subcategory and how they are performing overall.

You can also look at the reviews of similar books. Generally, the more reviews left on places like Amazon, the more the book was purchased and read. Not every reader will leave a review, so having a good number of reviews for any given book shows that it is something that has reached a target audience multiple times. Pay attention to three star reviews. These reviews will generally give you feedback on the things that the author missed in their book and give you an idea for what the target audience is looking for. Maybe the author didn't thoroughly explain a subject or maybe there was an element left out that the reader was looking for. Sometimes this happens in fiction books when a reader wants more than what was provided in the novel. This will help give you ideas of things you should try to include in your book.

Another thing to consider when selecting a niche is whether or not the niche has a flooded market. Writing a book in a flooded market will result in your work getting lost in the shuffle. If you're careful to keep an eye out for new niches that are just starting to become popular, you will have a better chance at being successful and creating a book that is not only needed in the market, but stands a better chance to get noticed by new people who are looking for books like yours. You can gauge how successful a new niche on the rise will be by looking at the reviews for the few books already available in that genre. Combining the reviews with the rankings will let you know what people think about the new niche and how many people are being drawn to the new niche. A good way to figure out what's going to be popular in the future is to pay attention to future release dates of things like movies or up and coming product releases.

Finding a new niche or an up and coming niche is especially critical for non-fiction books. Writing on a subject that has been well established with ample books and research already available may not be the best option unless you can provide a new twist on it. Again, take note of the reviews of the books currently on the market. Find out what things were missed in them and see what the readers need or are looking for when they purchase those books. Researching and analyzing the information already available will help you to come up with a new idea or a twist on an old one so that the readers will be engaged and drawn to your book over others already available on the market.

Be on the lookout for inspiration in all its forms. Take note of what's happening in the world around you. What are your friends and family sharing on social media? What major events are happening around the world? Are there any new movie releases that people are excited about? Researching and looking for day-to-day inspirations is only part of determining what you want to write about. At the end of the day, you should write about what you feel. If you're passionate about your topic, you'll be able to produce a quality book that's both engaging and entertaining to the reader and you'll find that the writing process will be a much smoother process.

CHAPTER THREE
CREATING AN OUTLINE

Once you have decided what topic you want to write about, the next step in the process is to sit down and outline your book. This will be one of the more important steps and will allow you to see the flow of your book from start to finish. This process is designed for you to work through your thoughts and organize the layout of your book.

To begin the process of designing an outline for your book, start by writing down a general idea of where you would like your book to begin and end. Once you know the path your book needs to take, you can plot out the middle. If you're writing an information book or a how-to book, write down what you want to accomplish by the end of the book. Then go back and consider your audience. If your target audience is for the everyday person who may not have any knowledge of what you're writing, then start at the beginning. Make a list of things you need to discuss to effectively communicate and explain the information you're trying to relay. With fiction and other types of books, you can start by plotting out what you want to happen in your book. Don't worry about filling in all the details. Just cover the major plot points. These plot points will be the topics that you need to cover in each chapter.

For example, if you're writing a book on how to paint your interior walls, you would start with thinking about what you are trying to accomplish by the end of your book. In the example, you're trying to teach the reader how to paint their interior walls. This is your end goal. From there, you need to list out a broad overview of the steps. An outline example is listed below:

Goal: Teach the reader how to paint their interior walls

1.   Picking out the right paint for the project

2.   Picking out the right tools for the job

3.   Preparing the room and walls for painting

4.   Painting the room

5.   Cleaning up

6.   Maintenance

7.   Conclusion

After you've settled on the major talking points that you need to cover in your book, go through each step and come up with a few highlights or details that you want to include under that chapter heading. This step might seem a bit tedious, but it helps to keep you on track. It also helps you when you feel stuck on an idea or plot point because you can refer to your outline to remind you of what you wanted to cover in that chapter. Continuing with the example above:

Goal: Teach the reader how to paint their interior walls

1.   Picking out the right paint for the project

    a.   Primers

    b.   Paint

   c.   Paint and primers in one

   d.   Flat, gloss, etc.

2. Picking out the right tools for the job

   a.   Types of rollers

   b.   Roller extensions

   c.   Tape

   d.   Brushes

3. Preparing the room and walls for painting

   a.   Removing items

   b.   Covering items

   c.   Cleaning walls

   d.   Taping the room

4. Painting the room

   a.   Technique

   b.   Covering the edges

5. Cleaning up

   a.   Brush and roller cleaning

   b.   Paint storage

6. Maintenance

   a.   Touch ups

   b.   Paint durability and proper cleaning

7. Conclusion

    a. Summarize the steps

    b. Provide recommendations on where to buy paint and tools

The details added to the outline should be short and to the point. You can add more information as you write the book. If you decide to make changes to your outline while you're writing your book, be sure that those changes won't affect the remainder of your outline. It is perfectly acceptable to make changes to your outline as you begin the writing process. Try not to focus too much on changing and perfecting your outline. Constantly changing things until you have the perfect outline can detract from the overall writing process. Remember, this is a tool that should help you keep track of your ideas and thoughts not hinder the writing process itself. When done correctly, the outline will keep you organized and assist you later in the process when you're writing blurbs or overviews of your book for publication. The outline will also be a good reference tool if you write additional books that are related. You will have an instant overview of what information you've covered in the first book and help you plan the next book. This is particularly useful for fiction writers who have multiple books in a series and rely on details from each book to continue with the next story.

Chapter Four
Character Development

Character development generally applies to fiction although it can also apply to non-fiction. Non-fiction books that would require character development are books written to tell a story that involves real events with real people. A biography, an autobiography, and a book detailing historical events or memoirs are just a few examples of non-fiction books that require character development. Books that are categorized as fiction usually center around a main character or set of main characters, making character development an extremely important part of the story. Failure to develop a character properly or using the wrong voice can result in the story being flat and you run the risk of losing the interest of the reader.

There are a few things to consider when developing a character. You can start by giving your character a name. Assign a history to them. Realize that they are made to mimic real people if you are writing fiction and are real people if you are writing a non-fiction book. They should be three dimensional with their own thoughts, feelings, and history. Visualize your character or characters. What is their hair color? What is their eye color? How tall are they? What kind of clothes do they like to wear? Do they have any bad habits? What about their family? What was their childhood like or if they're a child, what is their day-to-day life like? Do they have a favorite food? These details may not be relevant to your story and they may not even be mentioned in your story, but they will help you to create a character that comes off as real to the reader and will come in handy when you're writing and trying to figure out how your character or characters react to certain scenarios. If you create believable characters, your readers will be more likely to believe your story and they will be more engaged and invested in the characters and what happens to them throughout the story.

Part of character development is deciding what kind of voice to use throughout the book. There are three main types of voices: first person, second person, and third person. Again, each one comes with its own set of benefits and drawbacks.

First person point of view is an extremely limited point of view. It generally follows one character and the story is essentially told through their eyes. You will often find pronouns such as 'I' and 'we.'. Think of it as though your reader was inside your character's head. The character's thoughts, feelings, and actions would be known to the reader, but you would be limited in only using that person's perspective to tell the story. When using first person, you can switch points of view to another character; however, this is generally frowned upon because it can be confusing to the reader. It is difficult to keep track of whose head they're in as they read the story. A great way to accomplish writing first person point of view from multiple character's points of view is to use chapter breaks to switch points of view. Starting each chapter by indicating which character the story is being told from will let the reader know ahead of time and it won't be so jarring as they read through the story. An example of first person point of view is listed below:

I was vaguely aware of the room full of people staring at me. I could only focus on the man in front of me. "Here," I said as I handed him the note I had written for him. He flashed me a smile and my heart melted. No one could make me feel this way. I felt as though I were sixteen again.

Second person point of view is not commonly used in fiction. It involves using pronouns such as 'you' and 'your'. Second person point of view is where the narrator tells the story to you or is telling the story to another character. An example of second person point of view is this guide. The narrator of this story is speaking directly to you, the reader, and informing you on the contents of this book. Second person point of view narrative is also used in other medias such as movies and plays. Below is a written example of what writing in second person point of view narrative would look like:

What I am about to tell you is a story that is filled with heartache and sorrow. It is a story that will bring you near tears and feel as though your heart has been ripped from your chest. It is a story about love and the pain that comes with losing it.

Last on the list is third person point of view. Third person point of view comes in two forms: limited and omniscient. When writing in third person point of view, you will use pronouns such as 'he,' 'she,' and 'they' and generally avoid using pronouns such as 'I' and 'you' when directly speaking to the reader or when two characters are not actively engaged in dialogue.

Third person limited point of view is commonly used in fiction writing and is predominately used as an industry standard with publishing companies. Therefore, it is important to research your market before deciding on the type of book you want to write. If you are considering going through a publishing company for your book, then looking at their publication guidelines and restrictions will prevent you from having to redo your work to fit their guidelines. Each publishing house is different. Some will allow first person point of view narrative. Others will want you to strictly adhere to third person limited point of view narrative. Similarly, head hoping is generally frowned upon, but in some cases, it may be useful and allowed by the publisher.

With third person limited point of view, you are writing as a character telling the story from only their point of view. They are limited in how they see the world created by the writer and the thoughts and feelings of other characters can only be inferred through action or if the other characters have explicitly told the character that you are using as the narrative. One of the best things about third person limited point of view is it keeps the story consistent, allows more freedom in how the story is told by the writer, and you can change points of view. This is done usually by a scene break or chapter break. When you change points of view, the writing style is still third person limited, but you have changed from one character to another. Often, authors will do this when they need to show something that is happening off screen to their main character.

Authors will also use third person limited point of view narrative to do what is known as head hopping. Head hopping is a talent developed in writing. If you are unfamiliar with how to do this correctly, it is advised to research it and perfect your technique before attempting it in your book. Generally, head hopping is preferable to romance. This is because the focus is the relationship and when switching between the characters involved in the relationship, it is not jarring to the reader so long as they know whose head they are in at all times. It is important to understand that head hoping from a main character's head to a secondary character is not usually acceptable within the same scene. If you need to show a secondary character's thoughts or feelings, then it is best to have a scene break and give that character their own space to tell their story. The reason for this is because usually the secondary character's motivations and feelings do not coincide with the main characters and if you are writing romance, the secondary character is not involved in the relationship. Showing their point of view at the same time as the main characters often creates confusion and becomes distracting to the reader.

Recently, many publishing companies have started to shy away from head hopping so make sure this is a style that is applicable to your story and will benefit you in the future, not hinder your ability to get published later. If you are uncomfortable with head hopping, try limiting the scene to just one character's point of view. There are always additional ways to show other characters' thoughts and feelings within a scene. An example of third person limited point of view narrative is shown below:

Jake stared at the ceiling, thinking over every possible mistake he'd made on his most recent calculus test. The sound of his dorm room door opening drew his attention and he sat up to see who was entering his room. A familiar smile greeted him as his best friend, Peter, walked in and closed the door behind him. "How do you think you did?" Peter asked. Jake hesitated. He'd studied as much as he could but he still felt like it wasn't enough.

Third person omniscient point of view narrative is written from an all-seeing narrator. The easiest way to remember the difference between third person limited point of view and third person omniscient point of view is to consider each perspective. Limited means that you are limited to just one character at a time. Omniscient is more like telling the story through the eyes of a god. The narrator can see all character's emotions, actions, thoughts, and motives. This writing style is not as common in a lot of modern fiction. One of the reasons is because this writing style is one of the hardest to master and pull of in a manner that keeps the reader engaged in the book without jarring them every time the narrator hops from character to character. Many writers often confuse this with head hopping, but third person omniscient point of view is not the same as third person limited which can include multiple character's points of view even within the same scene. Third person omniscient point of view is a subjective perspective. It can often create a distance between the reader and the characters. With third person omniscient point of view narrative, the narrator is telling the story more than showing it. When the omniscient narrator is conveying the feelings and emotions of a character it is more like facts being stated to the reader than inferring strong emotions. An example of third person omniscient point of view narrative is shown below:

> *There were two people sitting in the room. Josh and Brandon sat across from one another, playing a game of chess as they discussed their activities earlier in the day. "I stopped by the memorial today," Josh said.*
>
> *Brandon looked up at him, worry showing on his face. Josh hadn't been back to the memorial since the incident. Josh had been afraid of seeing the images of his lost friends hung up on the wall for everyone's entertainment and he tended to avoid the area whenever they went for their usual walk. However, Josh had decided it was time to face his fear. He'd managed to spend the day looking at the people he'd lost without succumbing to the fear that had plagued him for so long.*

Whether you decide to write in third person limited, third person omniscient, second person, or first person point of view narrative will depend on your story and the characters that speak to you. Try to weigh the benefits of each one as well as their limitations. If you are uncomfortable with a new style that you want to try out, experiment with the new style by writing some practice scenes. Read back through the new style after you've finished and see if it conveys what you're trying to tell the reader and if the style does so in a manner that keeps the reader invested in the story.

The last thing to consider when telling the story and developing your character's voice is the tense in which you tell the story. Some writers will use a more present tense voice as though the actions were happening as the reader is reading the book. Other authors will use a more past tense voice to show that the story has already happened. Past tense is usually preferred because it isn't jarring to the reader. The reason present tense writing style is more jarring is because that is not usually how we tell stories. Even in our everyday writing or retelling of events that happened on social media etc., we use a past tense variation. Present tense is still acceptable, but make sure you read through your writing and find that it supports your story and is the voice you want to tell your story in.

Chapter Five
Writing the Book

You've got your idea. You've done your research. You've completed your outline and you have your character's developed. Now, it is time to begin the actual writing process. This can be difficult if you have a lot of distractions around. Writing requires self-discipline and dedication to the project. You need to be self-motivated to complete the book in a timely manner and this is where the outline that you made will come in handy. It will keep you on track and help motivate you so that you can tackle one idea or chapter at a time.

Writing is just like anything else, you need to schedule it and stick to that schedule. Don't let yourself get distracted. If you find it difficult to write at home because you can't seem to block out the day-to-day noises or interruptions, consider picking another spot to write. Things like the television, other people coming in and out of your room to ask you questions or to get items might seem like they are no big deal, but that can quickly eat up a lot of the time you've allocated to writing. This can be resolved by setting aside a designated time when you know you will have the space free to yourself.

If this isn't an option, you can always find a place outside of your home to work. Consider places close by. There are lots of coffee shops and stores with seating areas available for people who need to work. If these spots seem too crowded to you or if you have an odd schedule, get creative. McDonalds is usually open twenty-four hours a day and most places have Wi-Fi available to customers. The important thing to remember is to pick a spot that makes you feel comfortable. If none of the places suggested work for you, you can always try a park, a lake if you live near one, or a hiking trail. The isolated areas can help to inspire you and allow you the quiet you need to sit down with your thoughts and work. If you don't want to travel far away from home, you can always pick a spot in your own backyard or on your porch. Sometimes the change in scenery will help motivate you. The less distracted you are by what's going on around you, the easier it will be to finish what you need to get done.

Picking the perfect spot isn't the only thing that's important. You should also plan ahead. Creating a schedule for you to follow will not only motivate you finish your book, but it will allow you to check off items as you complete them, set deadlines, and have a projected timeframe of when you are able to get your book done. Be realistic. You don't have to rush to the finish line. Setting a schedule that you're able to stick to is more important than setting up a schedule that you can't keep. It will not only disappoint you every time you aren't able to complete the tasks you need to get done, but it can quickly make you frustrated and annoyed every time you sit down to work.

A schedule will also allow you to meet your deadlines. Sometimes these deadlines are our own personal goals or they might be on the time frame set by a publisher. Being able to meet those deadlines and prioritize your work will prevent you from rushing everything last minute to finish your work.

If you follow these guidelines during the writing process, then you will be able to avoid delays and roadblocks that could derail your work. It's important just to write. You need to get your thoughts onto the paper. That's the purpose of this step. You should try to avoid editing as much as possible. Every sentence doesn't have to be perfect. You will have a chance to fix things later and stopping to edit while writing not only slows down your writing process, but it can even result in you not finishing the book. As an editor, people are often highly critical of their work. They stress about each word on the page and it is very easy to get caught up in rewriting sentences repeatedly until you eventually lose the thread of what it is you were talking about. Avoiding editing during the writing process is something that all writers struggle with. Successful writers have managed to overcome their need to perfect and focus on getting their ideas to paper.

If filling in the details of your outline and sitting down to write everything needed for publication seems like a daunting task or is something you don't have the time to do, you can always hire a ghost writer. Ghost writers are people that you pay to write your book for you. This can save you time and can be inexpensive if you know what you're looking for. A good writer will be able to churn out roughly 900 words every hour. This may be more or less depending on the content, how creative you want them to be, if research is involved, and the type of writing you are wanting from them. A great place to look for ghost writers is through third-party sites like Freelancer or Upwork. There are many self-employed individuals who make their living by writing. Some of these individuals even have experience with publishing their own works and can often provide samples of some of the books they have published or worked on.

When looking for a ghost writer, consider their background. Look at their portfolio and make sure their style is what you want. If your book is about a highly-specialized area, you should also consider their background. For example, if you're trying to find someone to write a book on medical procedures, picking out a writer with a background in the medical field might be a better option than someone who has no background in the medical field.

There are many factors that go into the overall pricing of the book. A good author will charge at least a penny a word. Others may charge less, but might not produce a piece that you are completely happy with. Depending on what your book is about, you might have to pay someone even more than a penny a word. If you are requiring them put in extra work such as research, a round of edits, or other additional services, they may factor those things into their price. Keep in mind that you are working together to create your book and selecting the right person for the job is extremely important. Choosing someone with an established history is a great option. The experienced writers are used to working with deadlines and they generally have knowledge on how certain things should be formatted or written. If you have additional questions, you can even hire them as an advisor for tips and insight on the publishing industry and how to successfully brand your book.

When dealing with ghost writers, always draw up a contract or have it in writing somewhere stating that you are the owner of the piece. Even though it is a ghost writer working for you, you are the one who created the idea and if your intention is to publish the piece either through a publishing company or self-publishing, then you will need to own the copyright. Establishing this upfront will prevent messy legal implications down the road should they arise.

Keeping a schedule, finding a good place that motivates you to write, pushing through to meet your deadlines, and turning off your inner editor will ultimately lead you to a finished piece. If the writing process is something you want to avoid all together, then for a reasonable fee you can pay someone to fill in the details for you. Having a finished piece whether through your own writing or using the services of a ghost writer is the end goal you have been working towards. Remember that this is only the beginning process. Try not to focus on the details as you write. Everything can be changed or perfected later. The important thing is to have a completed manuscript and what will be known as the first draft of your book.

Chapter Six
The Editing Process

Once you've written your book, you can begin the process of working through technical edits and content edits. There are several ways to approach the editing process and the level of detail you'll need to spend on each item may vary. If your end goal is to go through a publishing company for publication, then minimal edits should be done for major issues such as typos and formatting restrictions. This is because the cost of editing is usually built in as a service they offer in exchange for getting a portion of your royalties. You are paying them for the service. Some people prefer to do full rounds of editing before submitting their manuscript to a publisher. This is perfectly acceptable as well. This will allow you to present your piece in the best manner possible, but it could afford you delays on submitting your completed manuscript for consideration.

If you opt to go through the editing process before submitting your manuscript to a publishing company for consideration or if you are going to self-publish your manuscript, then you'll have to tackle both content editing and technical editing. You can hire someone to help you edit your book or you can tackle the process yourself. Hiring an outside editor is always recommended because they can see things that you will miss and offer feedback on how your story reads as an outside perspective. If your resources are limited, then editing your book yourself will save you on the cost.

To begin the process of editing your manuscript yourself, start by reading the book out loud several times. This might be a lengthy process, but hearing how your words sound will help you pinpoint errors. Hearing your work can help you find grammatical errors, especially as it relates to using the right tense consistently throughout your book, and odd placed words that serve no purpose in the sentence. Verb tense is something that writers mix up. It's very easy to switch tenses when writing and it's important to be consistent throughout the entire manuscript. If you decide to go with a variation of past tense, make sure all internal dialogue and descriptions are written in a manner that is consistent with the tense you chose. If you use a variation of present tense, double check that you aren't switching to a past tense voice during descriptions and internal thoughts.

As you read through your manuscript, it might be easier to focus on content edits first and then focus on technical edits during another read through. If you're using a program like Microsoft Word, you can turn on a feature called track changes. This will show you a mark up of the things you've changed like printing out the manuscript and editing by hand. You can also leave comments for yourself if you're unsure about a scene or want to mark it for reference later.

Content editing is the process that involves reviewing the content of your manuscript. You're not focusing on the grammar or the spelling. You're strictly focusing on the content of your book. While reading through your manuscript, ask yourself, are there any plot holes? Was there anything that you didn't explain properly? Did you leave out any important details? Does the information you're giving the reader serve a purpose and is it understandable? Reading through your manuscript several times will help you answer these questions. The first read through will point out major issues. After you've fixed those, go back through and re-read the manuscript. Do the changes fit with the story and did they solve the problems you identified during the first read through? The last read through will hopefully require minimal changes and give you a better idea of how your finished piece will read.

Technical editing requires just one or two read throughs. As you read the manuscript in the technical editing process, pay careful attention to details of spelling, punctuation, and consistent use of titles. If you capitalize a title, make sure that the title is capitalized throughout the manuscript or follows the rules of editing for the style you are using. If you are formatting certain scenes such as italicizing internal dialogue, then double check that this was done for all internal dialogue scenes. Technical edits don't require a lot of time, but they do require a sharp eye.

If you can't afford to pay for an editor, then you might also consider giving your manuscript to friends or family and letting them read through it. You also have the option of getting a beta reader. A beta reader is someone who isn't a professional, but is willing to read through your drafts and help you with suggestions or comments in exchange for being able to read your book for free. A beta reader is usually found through contacts or fans willing to take time to help you.

You can ask your family, friends, or beta readers to make comments or leave their own edits through an editing program like Microsoft Word's track changes feature. Keep an open mind. You are asking them for their opinion. It may be difficult to handle criticism at first, but it is a learning process and should not be a reflection on you as a person. There will be times when you disagree with someone else's edits. That is okay. If it is a publishing house, you can usually message the editor for further explanation on why they think something needs to change or let them know why you think it should stay the same. At the end of the day, whether it is friends and family or a professional editor, they are all working to make your manuscript better. Take the positive feedback as well. Don't just dwell on the negatives. Nobody is perfect and don't let the need to fix things or change things stop you from writing in the future.

If you have the means, you can hire your own professional editor. Editors will often offer their services as a freelancer and can be found online. There are expensive companies that will charge you quite a large sum to edit your piece. It is usually best to avoid those since the cost will not outweigh the benefit you receive from their services unless they are providing additional services with the editing process. You can find freelance editors through sites like Freelancer, Upwork, and Fiverr. They usually charge a small fee per word and most will offer multiple rounds of editing. To hire an editor from either Freelancer, Upwork, or Fiverr, simply create an account and post a project.

Regardless of whether you choose to tackle the edits by yourself, employ your friends and family or a beta reader, or hire a professional, this is your chance to perfect your manuscript. You may find you have many edits or changes needed to make your manuscript into a finished product that you're happy with. There maybe times you disagree with the comments or recommended changes and that is acceptable. Try to view your book objectively and analyze it as though you weren't the one to write the book. You may struggle with the harsh critique, but keep in mind that this is to make your book better and not a personal jab at you or your writing. Every author must go through an editing process and it will only make you a better writer.

CHAPTER SEVEN

BOOK TITLE AND BOOK COVER

With a completed manuscript, you're almost ready for publication. You can choose to self-publish the book or you can go through a publishing house. Both come with benefits and drawbacks. If you've decided on self-publishing, you'll need to create a book cover and book title. These two things can be a deciding factor in how your book will be recognized by both readers and the search ability of the internet.

Choosing a book title is something that should have a lot of thought put into it. Don't just go with the first thing that sounds good. Consider what your story is about, the genre you want to market it in, and other book titles within that genre. A book title can greatly impact your marketability and the number of copies you will sell. Choosing the right words in your title is not only necessary to be successful, but also crucial in how your customers will perceive your book. The first thing a customer sees is your title and book cover so make them memorable.

Book Title and Cover for Traditional Publishing

If you plan on seeking out a publisher for your book, the book title and book cover process will be completely different than if you decide to self-publish. When you write for a publisher, you will have a team of people to help you through the process. Therefore, choosing the right publisher is important. Your publisher will generally be responsible for marketing your book, designing your book cover, and the distribution of your book. They need to be knowledgeable in the area you're writing in to appropriately market and sell your book.

When you choose a title, you should focus on capturing the essence of your book and picking something that grabs the attention of the publishing company. This is important because when you submit your manuscript, your title and description are the first things a publishing company will see. Picking out something that is catered to their interests will work in your favor because it draws the attention of the editor who will ultimately decide if your book is something they would like to publish. Focus on being creative and capturing what your book is about more than picking something that will be easy to market. If your publisher later decides that they need to change it, they will work with you to do so.

When selecting a book cover for a book that is going through a publishing company, often the publishing company will send you a survey asking you what you would like to see on the cover. Keep it simple. It's more important that the overall composition of the cover looks good than it is to include every detail you want envisioned. If there are important characteristics such as a main character with tattoos, include those details, but allow the artist freedom to fit what works best onto the cover. They have experience in this area and will often create something that will help your book sell. If they ask for information on what your book is about, include as much detail as possible for the artist. The artist usually doesn't read through your book before creating the cover and most of what they see will be what is given to them from the survey. Letting the artist know the genre and your target audience helps them to research what is currently popular in that market and pick key elements that help your book sell more copies.

Book Title for Self-Publishing

The book industry has a large market and a strong online presence. Creating a title that stands out can make the difference between success and failure in the large industry especially as a self-published author. The biggest difference between self-published authors and authors going through a traditional publishing company is the need to pick a title that will help you market your book since you're responsible for all the marketing if you choose not to hire someone to help you with that process. Your book title will depend upon the genre you're writing in. Things to consider when choosing the right book title are the intrigue factor of the book title, discoverability of the book, and choosing a title that is informative. For fiction authors, choosing a title that is intriguing and genre mesh should be considered above the others when deciding a book title.

Intriguing titles require creativity and knowing the genre of your book. Don't make the title so farfetched that it isn't relatable to your genre or something that doesn't adequately describe your book. Remember, you aren't just focusing on picking a title that sounds good. You are also focusing on how the title relates to your book. Drawing in the wrong crowd and sending misleading information to customers results in bad reviews and unhappy customers. The point of making your book title intriguing is to make the reader immediately want to buy your book.

Discoverability applies to a reader's ability to find your book based on your title. Famous authors or relatively well known self-published authors do not have to worry about this as much because they can rely on their name and previously published books to support their new releases. As a new author or an author without a large following, you should be more cautious in your selection. To make your book more discoverable, choose a title that is to the point. For example, if you're writing a book on how to decorate a cake, consider naming the book "How to Decorate a Cake." The title is to the point and will more than likely be what your readers search for when looking for information on how to decorate a cake. It also demonstrates that it has the answer to their specific question without them having to look too hard or rely on reviews to see if the book contains their desired information.

Genre mesh is a big issue for fiction writers. Crossing genre boundaries with book titles can lead to a misrepresented book and result in people purchasing your book who may not be into the genre you are writing. This can lead to negative reviews and will keep your book from reaching your target audience. Try to pick genre specific titles.

When it's all said and done, don't forget to do research. Find out what common and popular book titles are in the genre you're writing in. Avoid using common titles. These will have a lot of competition in the search engines and may leave your book grouped in with the numerous other books that share your title. Complicated titles won't be easy to remember and might not give enough clear information to accurately showcase your book. Use the information you find from books in your genre and change them into something that's simple, creative, and unique. It is much more important that your title be effective than it is anything else.

Book Cover for Self-Publishing

After you have a title picked out, your next task is to create a book cover. The book cover is an artistic representation of your book. There are free tools like Canva that help you create a book cover with the right dimensions. Some sites like Amazon require a certain set of dimensions or file size and these can be easily adjusted in Canva. You'll probably need some stock photos. These can be purchased for a small fee or you can search through some of the free ones offered on other sites. You need to make sure you have the rights to use them for your book before you manipulate them for your cover.

To get an idea of what your cover should look like, browse through some of the popular books in your genre. Take note of what is eye catching and replicate the feel with your own book cover. If you feel uncomfortable in designing your own book cover, you can always higher a freelancer to help with the process. Compile a list of what kinds of covers you like and let them know what elements you want to include on your cover. Some genres do better using a person on the cover while other genres have more success with symbols. Doing your research of the top selling books in your genre will help you to decide what is right for your book.

When creating a book cover, avoid using fonts that aren't easy to read. You can get creative by changing the font to emphasize a certain keyword in the title or by adding a splash of color to the text. Blend elements together so that the cover has a consistent composition. Avoid using too many design elements. You must find the right balance between the text you're showcasing and the imagery you're trying to capture for your book. Remember that a book cover and book title are the first things your readers will see. Make it count.

CHAPTER EIGHT
FORMATTING AND ROYALTIES

Formatting and Self-Publishing

Your book isn't finished until it is published. If you're self-publishing, you'll need to format it so that it is in the appropriate form for distribution. Amazon, for example, requires your book to be converted into their format before you can publish it on their website. This is due to the nature of their Kindle software and how they deliver the books to their readers.

Formatting your book for Kindle can range for simplistic to complicated. It all depends on the type of book and what kind of features you have included in your book. If you have a lot of graphs and pictures, formatting your book will be significantly harder than if your book is composed mostly of plain text. Amazon does a pretty decent job at walking you through the steps. They recommend you save your file in Microsoft Word (DOC/DOCX) or HTML format.

Kindle eBooks are published through Kindle Direct Publishing. You will set up an author account and provide your tax information and bank information so that you can be paid. If you have an existing Amazon account, you can choose to use it. Once you've created your account and are signed in, you have the option of creating a Kindle eBook or paperback. If you click Kindle eBook, it walks you through the steps needed to publish your book. It asks you for the:

- Book title

- Subtitle

- Series title (if applicable)

- Author and contributors

- Description

- Publishing rights

- Keywords

- Categories

- Age range

It also asks whether you want to have the book set to be published at a future date and list the title for pre-order.

When considering your description, title, and subtitle, you want to choose words that optimize the search ability of your book. These words are commonly referred to as keywords and picking the right keywords could mean the difference between success and failure. Keywords allow the search engines on Amazon, Google, and other platforms to correctly associate your book with the search criteria entered into the search bar by your prospective customers. If you need help deciding on keywords, you can use many of the free SEO (Search Engine Optimization) keyword research tools. These tools help generate keywords that are commonly searched for based on your needs and show the competition as well as the search volume. A useful tool is Keyword Tool. It offers you the chance to research words specific to the search engine that you're most concerned with like Google or Amazon.

Keyword research tools will help you in deciding which keywords are too broad and which ones are too specific and not frequently searched for. When deciding on keywords, it is best to pick keywords that have high traffic and less competition. This improves the odds of your book being discovered and discovered by the right people. Keywords can be placed in your title, subtitle, summary, book cover's file name, meta data, and much more. Try to find long tail keywords. These are phrases and usually have less competition. Remember to keep it to the point so that it is also still searchable. An example of a long tail keyword is: "Romance Suspense Thriller." Be sure to review any guidelines given by Amazon when selecting your keywords.

Your book description is an excellent place to use keywords. It offers you a chance to include as many as you would like, but be careful. You can overuse this feature. It is nearly impossible to optimize your description to attract every keyword you want associated with your book. Instead, pick a few and get creative. It is just as important to have a description that grabs the reader's attention as it is to work in those keywords. Balancing the two will create a better overall description of your book. You'll find that your book is better optimized for search engines by picking the most important keywords and using them appropriately. The creative hook you use for your book is what keeps readers interested and hopefully lead to a sale.

Next, you'll be given instructions on uploading your completed manuscript. Most DOC/DOCX files convert well to eBooks and Amazon has created a previewer for you to use to make sure your book converted successfully. To help with the optimization of converting documents into eBooks, Amazon offers a set of instructions on what is needed. For print books, the requirements are stricter because the incorrect format could result in printing errors. If you feel uncomfortable with formatting your book, consider finding someone to format your book in accordance with Kindle standards on Fiverr.

If your book is relatively simple and doesn't have a lot of graphs or pictures, there are some things you can do to help with the conversion. If you want to create intentional page breaks for new chapters or scenes, be sure to use Microsoft Word's "Page Break" feature to create them. During the conversion, it registers an intentionally made page break and appropriately places the next chapter or scene on a new Kindle page. If you want to include pictures, Amazon recommends using Word's "Insert" function and warns against copying and pasting.

For KDP (Kindle Direct Publishing) you'll be asked to upload your manuscript separate from your cover. The cover will be added separately. Amazon has also integrated a new feature into their publishing system that allows you to create your cover using their "Cover Creator." Review your manuscript for formatting errors and when you are satisfied, proceed to uploading your book to Amazon.

Formatting your book for print requires some additional steps. Return to the "Bookshelf" section in your account and select the paperback option. This walks you through the necessary steps for creating a paperback book. For print books, Amazon recommends saving your file as a PDF. You can do this easily through Microsoft Word by using the "Save As" feature and changing the file type to PDF. Previously and more frequently used is CreateSpace. CreateSpace is affiliated with Amazon and is a member of the Amazon group of companies. They provide tools that help you with self-publishing and offer a "print on demand" service. This is a cheaper alternative to paying a printing servicer upfront for copies and trying to sell them. CreateSpace takes a portion of your sales for your print on demand book instead. They get paid when you get paid and they print the book when it is ordered so that there's no excess in printing costs. CreateSpace offers a royalty calculator for figuring out your percentage. It's based on your book and the price you list it for. Their royalty calculator can be found at:

https://www.createspace.com/Products/Book/

If you need to format your book into different formats, you might consider hiring someone to do the job. Often, they will give you a range of formats or create a version of your manuscript that integrates flawlessly with service providers such as Amazon. There are many different eBook formats available. Barnes and Noble require ePub for their eBook distribution. The ePub format is a bit more difficult to transcribe even using their conversion software that they provide. There are many companies that offer these services, but you can just as easily find someone via Freelancer, Fiverr, or Upwork willing to do it for much cheaper depending on the level of expertise needed to create these convertible versions.

Traditional Publishing

An alternative to self-publishing and one that is a bit more inclusive of certain features like formatting, book cover design, editing, distributions, and marketing is opting to go with a publisher. This process can vary from publisher. Make sure that you research publishing houses that interest you. Look at their royalty options, their commitment to the authors and the genre you are interested in. These things are important because it is a business agreement. You might be sending your manuscript to them for consideration, but you will also be giving them a large portion of your royalties in exchange for their services. Many publishing houses offer 40% or less royalties to authors. That means that the publisher will take more than 50% of the income derived from your book, so make sure they're offering comparable work that equates to greater than 50% of the work needed to promote, design, format, and edit your book.

To submit your manuscript to a publisher, you can visit their website. They usually have instructions on how to submit your manuscript. Some publishing houses do not accept previously published work. Self-publishing may or may not count to them, so be careful if you're wanting to switch from self-publish to going with a publishing house. Some publishers also require you to go through an agent and won't accept unsolicited manuscripts. Others might only accept manuscripts in a certain genre at the time you are looking to send yours.

If a publisher wants you to go through an agent, you need to find a reputable agent that works with that publisher. This can be a bit difficult because it requires good old fashion research. There's no quick list of people that work with the publishing houses. Oftentimes these agents have fees, including fees just to submit to them for consideration. Be careful of scams and thoroughly research an agent. Feel free to contact them, ask for references, and see their work. This might be an application process, but it's also a business arrangement and you have the right to know how your manuscript is handled, what they can offer you, and if they are a trustworthy source before sending them any kind of money or your manuscript. Your manuscript is your livelihood and you wouldn't want someone to steal it or your ideas and try to publish them as their own.

When you submit your manuscript to a publisher or an agent, they will ask for a query letter, which states various information about your manuscript, and a sample from your manuscript if not the whole script itself. The query letter is basically a way for you to sell the book to them. Usually, they'll want to know about you, your publication history, what the book is about, what genre is it, what's the title, how long is it, and why you think it would be a good fit for them. You'll need to be creative and professional when writing a query letter. You want it to be appealing to the editor or agent who reads it. If a publishing company or agent doesn't like the letter, they may never even open your manuscript.

If the publishing company wants you to submit a sample of your manuscript, check to see if they are requesting a certain sample size or if any sample will do. Some will want the first 1,000 words. If that is the case, carefully analyze those few pages and make sure they read in a manner that makes the editor or agent want to continue reading your book. Some publishers want a sample and a summary of your book. The summary lets them know what happens in the book and how it ends without the need for reading through the entire manuscript. Again, get creative. Make sure it is intriguing and interesting to read. Get a second or third opinion if you have any doubts. You want this to be the best representation of your work.

Royalties

If you choose to self-publish your book through services such as Amazon, you have higher earning potential, but you must do more of the work. Editing, creating a cover, and marketing is left up to you. You'll need to write a description for your book and make sure your book has a polished and professional finish. Self-publishing is quickly becoming a favorite among authors including authors who were previously successful with big name publishing houses. This is because as a self-published author you get to keep the rights to your book, your pen name, and decide where and how it will be presented.

With Amazon's Kindle Direct Publishing, you have two options. You can opt to publish it in a way that allows you to also upload your book to other platforms for purchase or you can enroll your book in KDP Select. KDP Select is a program that gives you the chance to earn even higher royalties and offers Kindle Unlimited enrollment. Kindle Unlimited is a subscription service Amazon provides customers where they pay a monthly fee to read books offered through Kindle Unlimited for free. As an author with a book offered through the system, Amazon divides the KDP Select Global Fund of profits received from their readers and disperses it between the authors who have their books enrolled. The amount that you receive of the share depends on how many pages were read by customers during the billing cycle. KDP Select also allows you to earn 70% royalty for sales to customers in Japan, India, Brazil, and Mexico and offers promotional tools such as countdown deals, time-bound promotional discounts, and free book promotions. The drawback to using KDP Select is that you can't publish your book on another platform.

Royalty options available for KDP are offered in a 35% royalty or 70% royalty commission. To be eligible for the 70% royalty option, your book must be priced between $2.99 and $9.99 and not part of public domain. The catch to the 70% commission rate is delivery costs will be subtracted before you get the calculated 70%. Delivery costs are estimated based on the file size of your book. Average delivery costs are $0.06 per unit sold. Many people have reported that for a 70,000 word book depending on the coding and formatting of the book could cost anywhere from

$.10 to $.45 per unit sold. The 70% commission is only eligible in certain countries although that list is extensive. It includes:

- Andorra

- Australia (including territories Christmas Island (CX), Cocos Keeling Islands (CC), Heard & McDonald Islands (HM), and Northfolk Island (NF))

- Austria

- Belgium

- Brazil*

- Canada

- France

- Great Britain

- Guernsey

- Germany

- Gibraltar

- India*

- Italy

- Ireland

- Isle of Man

- Japan*

- Jersey

- Lichtenstein

- Luxembourg

- Monaco

- Mexico*

- Netherlands

- New Zealand (including territories Cook Islands (CK), Niue (NU), and Tokelau)

- San Marino

- Switzerland

- Spain

- United Kingdom

- United States

- Vatican City

Digital books enrolled in KDP Select are the only ones eligible to receive 70% royalty for sales to customers in Brazil, Japan, Mexico, and India. If you choose the 35% option, you won't be charged deliver costs. Some people prefer this option if they have a large file with numerous pictures or charts or if they want to sell their book outside of the price limits set by Amazon. The 35% royalty option is comparable to what you would expect from a publishing company. While the 70% royalty is really appealing to authors. They get the control of their book without the limitations of a publishing house and get to earn more royalties on their sales.

A traditional publishing house averages between 3% and 40% net royalties for electronic print. Standard print is significantly less at about 6 to 10%. A publishing company may also offer advances in addition to a royalty package. Advances are money given up front to the author so that they don't have to wait for royalty payout. Very few publishing houses offer 40% net royalties. Most offer 25% and take 75% for their portion. This can pay out big time if it is a reputable publishing company that puts in 75% of the work. Those small numbers in royalties won't matter as much because the publishing company will work hard to market your book and give you larger exposure without you needing to put in much effort.

CHAPTER NINE
CONCLUSION

Creating, writing, editing, and publishing your book requires a lot of dedication and attention to detail. It will also require research and time. That's why it is important to create a schedule and plan your book before beginning the process. The planning and scheduling helps you keep your deadlines and enables you to work through the publishing process in a more efficient way. When you're finished with your manuscript, you can use your outline and planning materials to help you publish your book.

Nowadays, many readers enjoy both published books and self-published books. Publishing houses are often struggling to release books at the price that self-published authors can afford, making it hard to compete. They do have some advantages such as distributions to bookstores and a large fan base for some of their more popular authors, but self-publishing is on the rise. Authors are taking control of the writing process and learning more and more about how to market themselves and brand their books. To be successful at it, you'll need to master the writing process. Following the steps provided here will help you accomplish that goal and set you on the path to success. Whether you choose to self-publish your book or go through an agent or publishing company, it is important to remember that your book is worth the time and effort you put into it. Don't be afraid to advocate for you book, seek out advice, or try new things. Stick to the plan and create a system that works for you using the tools you've been given. In the end, you'll have a finished product that you can be confident will succeed.

BONUS

Do you want a free book that teaches you how to earn even more money?

If you answered YES, you're in the right place. Nowadays, everyone needs a little help making ends meet. The methods described in this book will work for anyone willing to put in the effort. But once rolling, passive income can be a ticket to the financial freedom you've always wanted. No more living paycheck to paycheck. No more scrounging for extra cash after the bills are paid. With the tools described in this book, it is possible to live debt free and even quit your full-time job.

Right now, you can get a FREE copy of Passive Recurring Income with Shopify. This book gives you all the tools you need to supplement your income. Go to this link for instant access: https://nicholalett.lpages.co/passive-income/

www.ingramcontent.com/pod-product-compliance
Lightning Source LLC
Chambersburg PA
CBHW070049260726

48658CB00002B/812